EVEN MORE SUNDAY SOLOS

FOR PIANO

PRELUDES, OFFERTORIES & POSTLUDES

ISBN 978-1-61780-376-5

HAL•LEONARD®
CORPORATION
7777 W. BLUEMOUND RD. P.O. BOX 13819 MILWAUKEE, WI 53213

Visit Hal Leonard Online at
www.halleonard.com

CONTENTS

ALPHABETICAL LISTING OF SONGS

ALL THINGS BRIGHT AND BEAUTIFUL

Words by CECIL FRANCES ALEXANDER
17th Century English Melody

With a classical feel

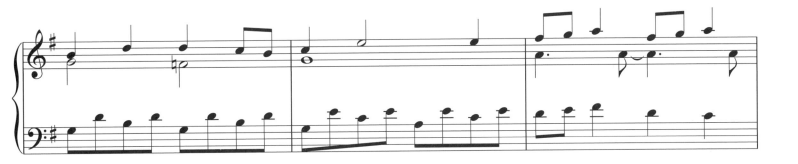

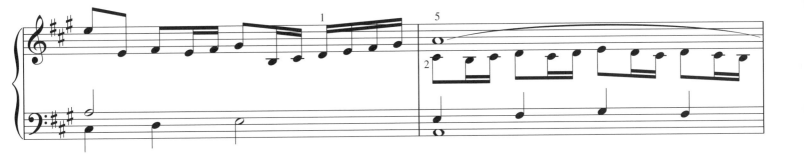

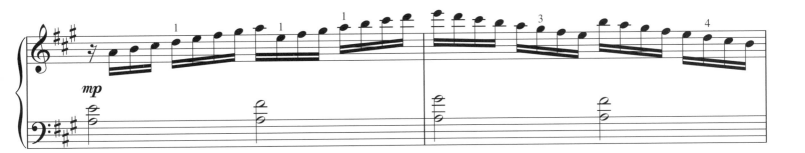

ANCIENT WORDS

Words and Music by
LYNN DeSHAZO

Moderately

With pedal

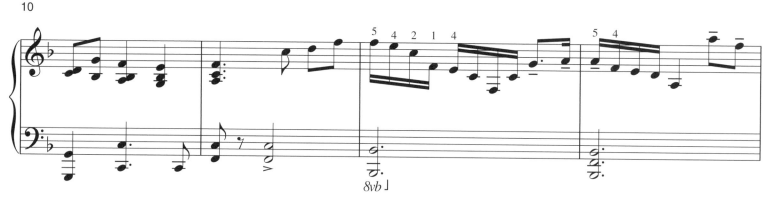

BRETHREN, WE HAVE MET TO WORSHIP

Words by GEORGE ATKINS
Music by WILLIAM MOORE

Moderately fast

COME THOU FOUNT, COME THOU KING

Traditional
Additional Words and Music by
THOMAS MILLER

With movement

IN THE GARDEN

Words and Music by
C. AUSTIN MILES

Reflectively

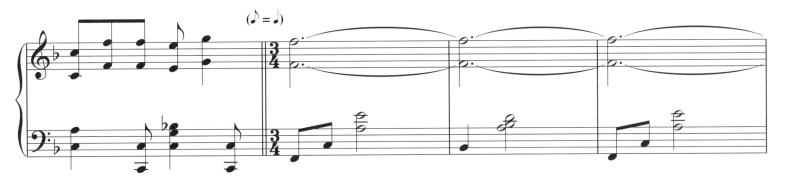

SPEAK O LORD

Words and Music by STUART TOWNEND
and KEITH GETTY

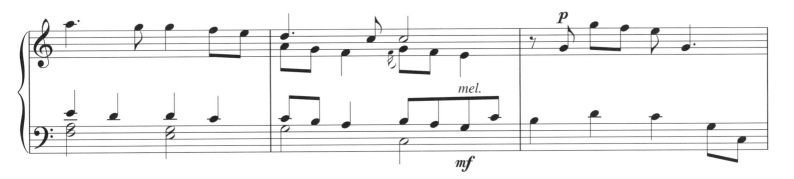

24

HOW GREAT IS OUR GOD

Words and Music by CHRIS TOMLIN,
JESSE REEVES and ED CASH

With praise

TAKE MY LIFE AND LET IT BE

Words by FRANCES R. HAVERGAL
Music by HENRY A. CÉSAR MALAN

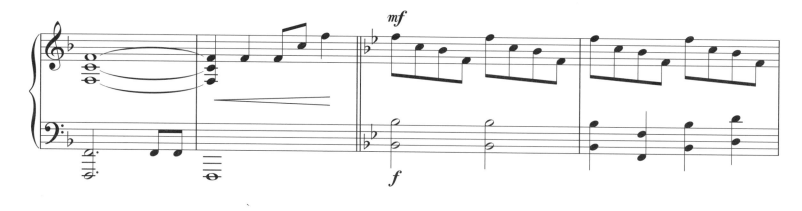

33

WE BOW DOWN

Words and Music by
TWILA PARIS

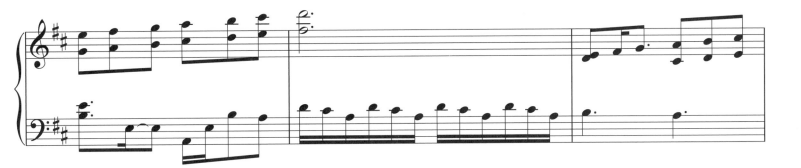

THIS IS MY FATHER'S WORLD

Words by MALTBIE D. BABCOCK
Music by FRANKLIN L. SHEPPARD

With expression

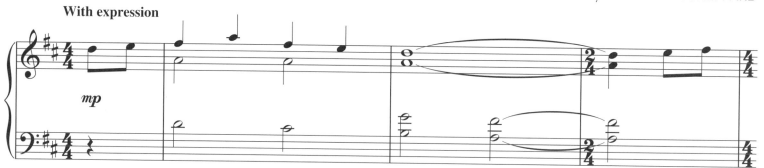

40

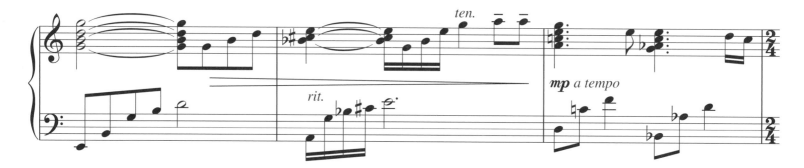

I GIVE YOU MY HEART

Words and Music by
REUBEN MORGAN

45

CHANGE MY HEART OH GOD

Words and Music by
EDDIE ESPINOSA

Flowing, with much expression

With pedal

I NEED THEE EVERY HOUR

Words by ANNIE S. HAWKS
Music by ROBERT LOWRY

Gently

With pedal

3

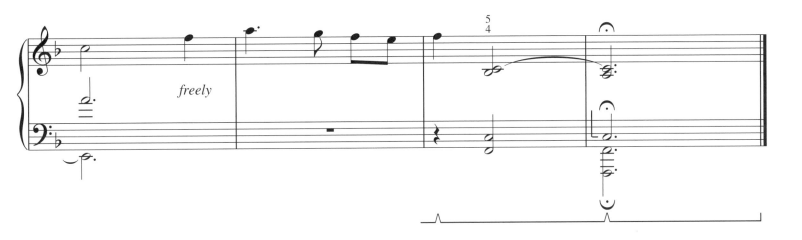

I WILL RISE

Words and Music by CHRIS TOMLIN,
JESSE REEVES, LOUIE GIGLIO
and MATT MAHER

Moderately

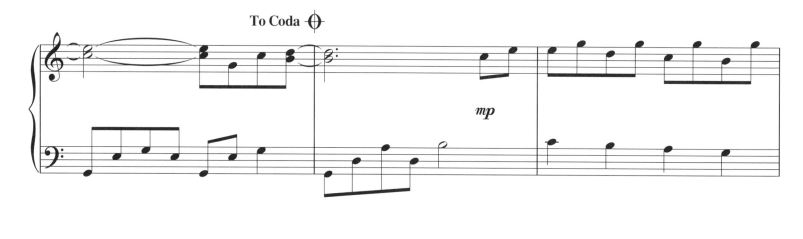

To Coda

D.S. al Coda

CODA

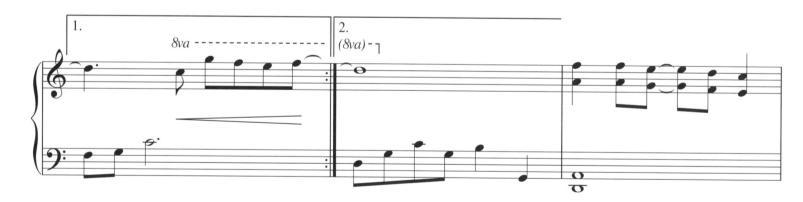

59

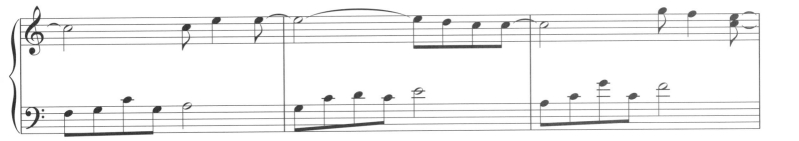

MY FAITH LOOKS UP TO THEE

Words by RAY PALMER
Music by LOWELL MASON

Warmly, with expression

With pedal

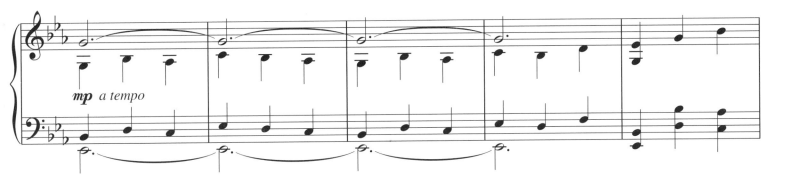

cresc. poco a poco

f

mp

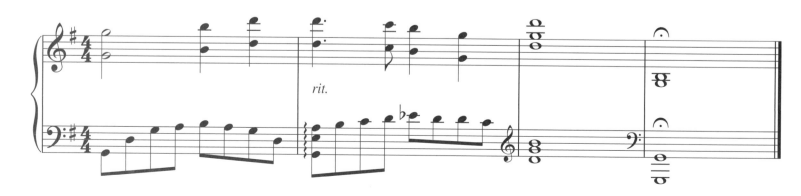

rit.

OFFERING

Words and Music by
PAUL BALOCHE

Moderately slow

SAVIOR, LIKE A SHEPHERD LEAD US

Words from *Hymns for the Young*
Attributed to DOROTHY A. THRUPP
Music by WILLIAM B. BRADBURY

Gently, with expression

WHAT A FRIEND WE HAVE IN JESUS

Words by JOSEPH M. SCRIVEN
Music by CHARLES C. CONVERSE

Reflectively, rubato

Slightly faster

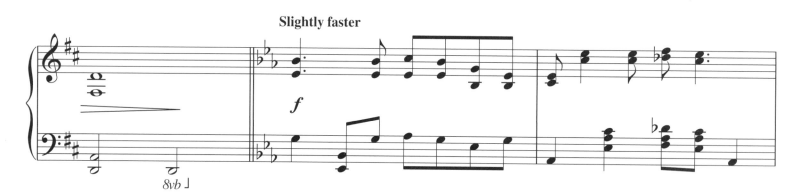

'TIS SO SWEET TO TRUST IN JESUS

Words by LOUISA M.R. STEAD
Music by WILLIAM J. KIRKPATRICK

Flowing, with much expression

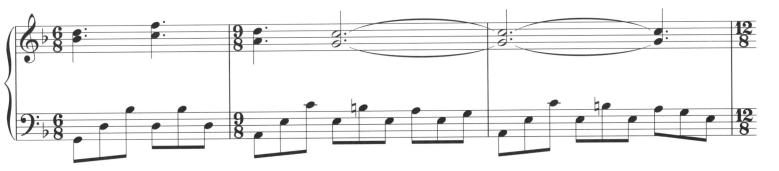

74

molto rit.

mp *a tempo*

dim.

pp

YOUR NAME

Words and Music by PAUL BALOCHE
and GLENN PACKIAM

Moderately

AWESOME GOD

Words and Music by
RICH MULLINS

Steady four

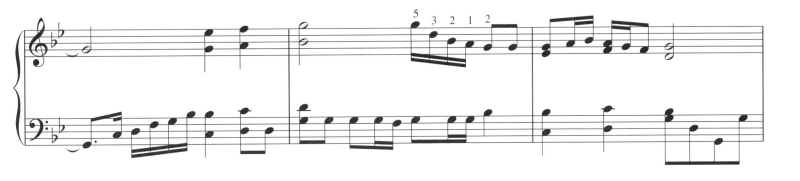

LEAD ON, O KING ETERNAL

Words by ERNEST W. SHURTLEFF
Music by HENRY T. SMART

84

Expressively, slightly slower

Broadly

THE CHURCH'S ONE FOUNDATION

Words by SAMUEL JOHN STONE
Music by SAMUEL SEBASTIAN WESLEY

Confidently

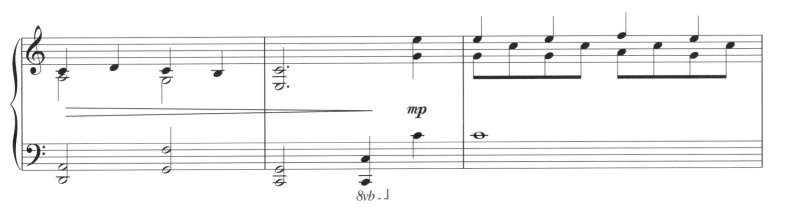

HOW FIRM A FOUNDATION

Words from John Rippon's *A Selection of Hymns*
Early American Melody

With strength

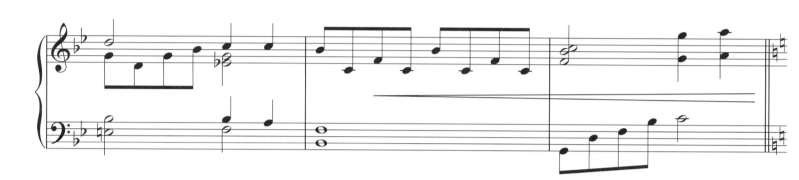

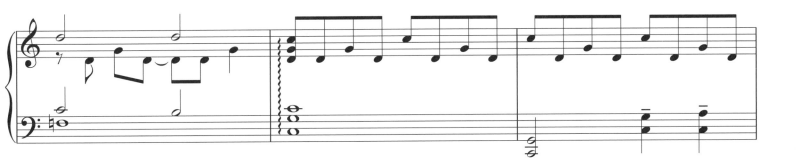

I LOVE THY KINGDOM, LORD

Words by TIMOTHY DWIGHT
Music from *The Universal Psalmodist*
Adapted by AARON WILLIAMS

With energy

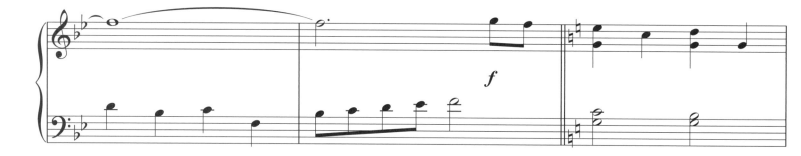

bring out melody

LORD, I LIFT YOUR NAME ON HIGH

Words and Music by
RICK FOUNDS

Joyfully

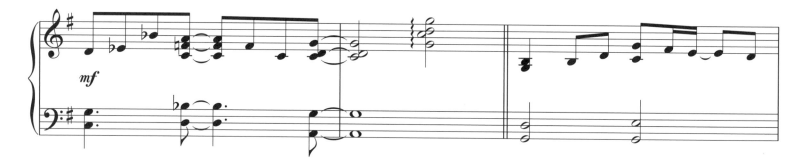

PRAISE HIM! PRAISE HIM!

Words by FANNY J. CROSBY
Music by CHESTER G. ALLEN

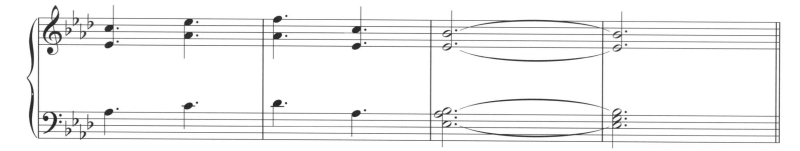

SING, SING, SING

Words and Music by CHRIS TOMLIN,
JESSE REEVES, DANIEL CARSON,
TRAVIS NUNN and MATT GILDER

Driving

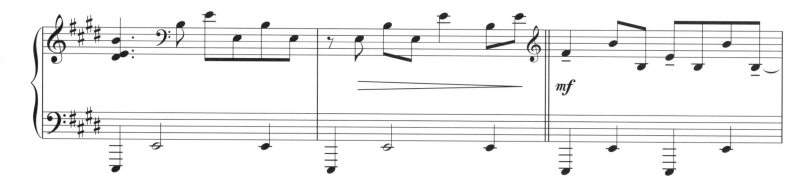

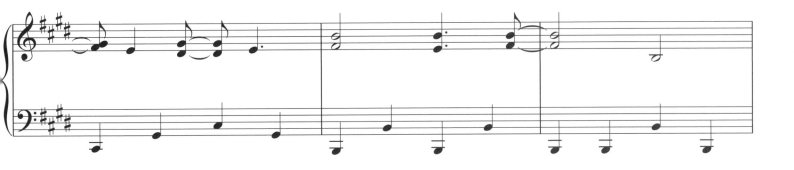

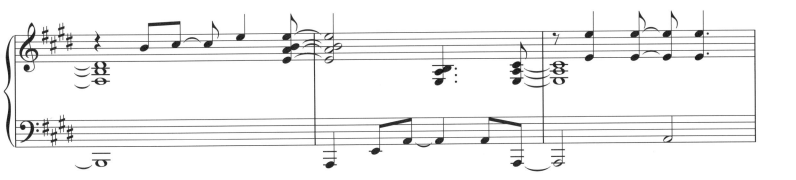

Slightly broader

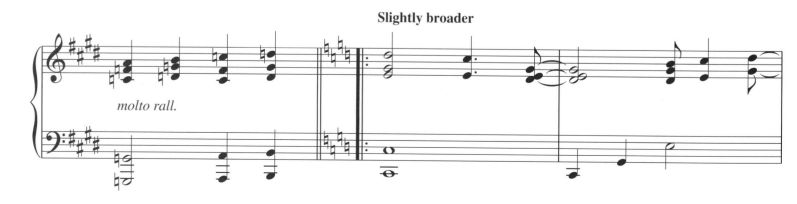

molto rall.

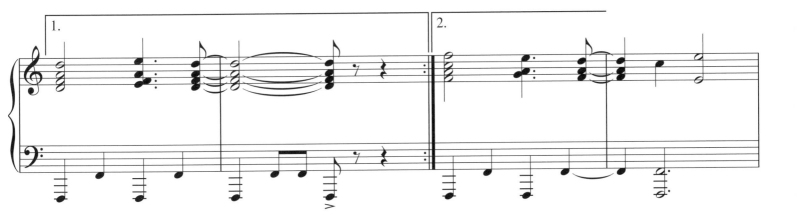

SOON AND VERY SOON

Words and Music by
ANDRAÉ CROUCH

Gospel style

broadening

rall.

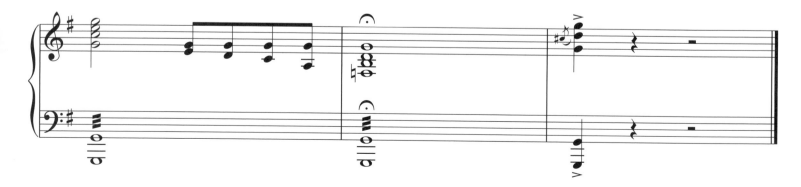

WORTHY OF WORSHIP

Words by TERRY YORK
Music by MARK BLANKENSHIP

With majesty

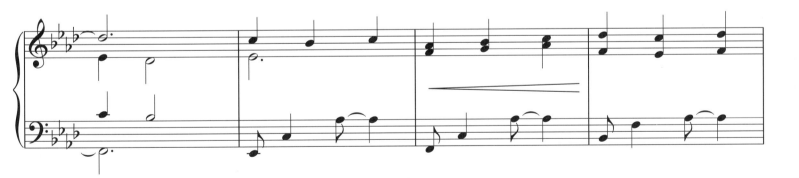

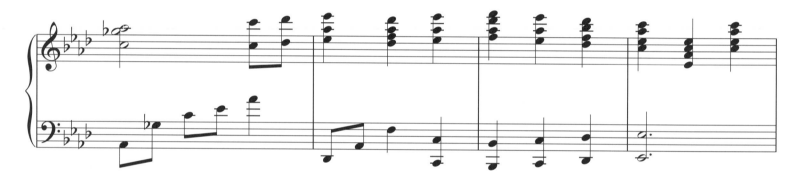

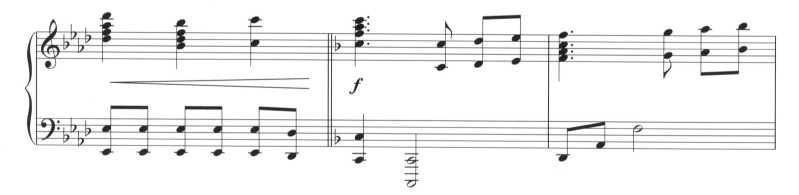

The Best
PRAISE & WORSHIP
Songbooks for Piano

Above All
THE PHILLIP KEVEREN SERIES
15 beautiful praise song piano solo arrangements by Phillip Keveren. Includes: Above All • Agnus Dei • Breathe • Draw Me Close • He Is Exalted • I Stand in Awe • Step by Step • We Fall Down • You Are My King (Amazing Love) • and more.
00311024 Piano Solo..................................$12.99

Blended Worship Piano Collection
Songs include: Amazing Grace (My Chains Are Gone) • Be Thou My Vision • Cornerstone • Fairest Lord Jesus • Great Is Thy Faithfulness • How Great Is Our God • I Will Rise • Joyful, Joyful, We Adore Thee • Lamb of God • Majesty • Open the Eyes of My Heart • Praise to the Lord, the Almighty • Shout to the Lord • 10,000 Reasons (Bless the Lord) • Worthy Is the Lamb • Your Name • and more.
00293528 Piano Solo $17.99

Blessings
THE PHILLIP KEVEREN SERIES
Phillip Keveren delivers another stellar collection of piano solo arrangements perfect for any reverent or worship setting: Blessed Be Your Name • Blessings • Cornerstone • Holy Spirit • This Is Amazing Grace • We Believe • Your Great Name • Your Name • and more.
00156601 Piano Solo $12.99

The Best Praise & Worship Songs Ever
80 all-time favorites: Awesome God • Breathe • Days of Elijah • Here I Am to Worship • I Could Sing of Your Love Forever • Open the Eyes of My Heart • Shout to the Lord • We Bow Down • dozens more.
00311057 P/V/G..................................$22.99

The Big Book of Praise & Worship
Over 50 worship favorites are presented in this popular "Big Book" series collection. Includes: Always • Cornerstone • Forever Reign • I Will Follow • Jesus Paid It All • Lord, I Need You • Mighty to Save • Our God • Stronger • 10,000 Reasons (Bless the Lord) • This Is Amazing Grace • and more.
00140795 P/V/G $24.99

Contemporary Worship Duets
arr. Bill Wolaver
Contains 8 powerful songs carefully arranged by Bill Wolaver as duets for intermediate-level players: Agnus Dei • Be unto Your Name • He Is Exalted • Here I Am to Worship • I Will Rise • The Potter's Hand • Revelation Song • Your Name.
00290593 Piano Duets $10.99

The Best of Passion
Over 40 worship favorites featuring the talents of David Crowder, Matt Redman, Chris Tomlin, and others. Songs include: Always • Awakening • Blessed Be Your Name • Jesus Paid It All • My Heart Is Yours • Our God • 10,000 Reasons (Bless the Lord) • and more.
00101888 P/V/G $19.99

Praise & Worship Duets
THE PHILLIP KEVEREN SERIES
8 worshipful duets by Phillip Keveren: As the Deer • Awesome God • Give Thanks • Great Is the Lord • Lord, I Lift Your Name on High • Shout to the Lord • There Is a Redeemer • We Fall Down.
00311203 Piano Duet..................................$12.99

Shout to the Lord!
THE PHILLIP KEVEREN SERIES
14 favorite praise songs, including: As the Deer • El Shaddai • Give Thanks • Great Is the Lord • How Beautiful • More Precious Than Silver • Oh Lord, You're Beautiful • A Shield About Me • Shine, Jesus, Shine • Shout to the Lord • Thy Word • and more.
00310699 Piano Solo $14.99

Sunday Solos in the Key of C
CLASSIC & CONTEMPORARY WORSHIP SONGS
22 C-major selections, including: Above All • Good Good Father • His Name Is Wonderful • Holy Spirit • Lord, I Need You • Reckless Love • What a Beautiful Name • You Are My All in All • and more.
00301044 Piano Solo $14.99

The Chris Tomlin Collection – 2nd Edition
15 songs from one of the leading artists and composers in Contemporary Christian music, including the favorites: Amazing Grace (My Chains Are Gone) • Holy Is the Lord • How Can I Keep from Singing • How Great Is Our God • Jesus Messiah • Our God • We Fall Down • and more.
00306951 P/V/G $17.99

Top Christian Downloads
21 of Christian music's top hits are presented in this collection of intermediate level piano solo arrangements. Includes: Forever Reign • How Great Is Our God • Mighty to Save • Praise You in This Storm • 10,000 Reasons (Bless the Lord) • Your Grace Is Enough • and more.
00125051 Piano Solo..................................$14.99

Top 25 Worship Songs
25 contemporary worship hits includes: Glorious Day (Passion) • Good, Good Father (Chris Tomlin) • Holy Spirit (Francesca Battistelli) • King of My Heart (John Mark & Sarah McMillan) • The Lion and the Lamb (Big Daddy Weave) • Reckless Love (Cory Asbury) • 10,000 Reasons (Matt Redman) • This Is Amazing Grace (Phil Wickham) • What a Beautiful Name (Hillsong Worship) • and more.
00288610 P/V/G $17.99

Top Worship Downloads
20 of today's chart-topping Christian hits, including: Cornerstone • Forever Reign • Great I Am • Here for You • Lord, I Need You • My God • Never Once • One Thing Remains (Your Love Never Fails) • Your Great Name • and more.
00120870 P/V/G $16.99

The World's Greatest Praise Songs
Shawnee Press
This is a unique and useful collection of 50 of the very best praise titles of the last three decades. Includes: Above All • Forever • Here I Am to Worship • I Could Sing of Your Love Forever • Open the Eyes of My Heart • and so many more.
35022891 P/V/G $19.99

HAL•LEONARD®

www.halleonard.com

P/V/G = Piano/Vocal/Guitar Arrangements

Prices, contents, and availability subject to change without notice.